# YOU KNOW YOU'RE
# OVER THE HILL
## WHEN...

Written By:
**Herbert Kavet**

Illustrated By:
**Martin Riskin**

Manufactured in the United States of America

30 29 28 27 26 25 24 23 22 21 20 19 18 17 16 15 14 13 12 11 10 9 8 7 6 5 4 3 2

**Ivory Tower Publishing Co., Inc.**
125 Walnut St., P.O. Box 9132, Watertown, MA 02272-9132
Telephone #: (617) 923-1111    Fax #: (617) 923-8839

# YOU'RE OVER THE HILL WHEN...

You are just starting to use your age to elicit extra services. You no longer feel funny when college-age people call you Mr. or Ma'am.

**YOU'RE OVER THE HILL WHEN...**

Getting a little action means your prune juice is working.

# YOU'RE OVER THE HILL WHEN...

You no longer have any illusions about making it big in your job.
You fantasize less and less about going into your own business.

# YOU'RE OVER THE HILL WHEN...

Your name appears on every mail order list in the country.

# YOU'RE OVER THE HILL WHEN...

You still feel your youthful ardor, but only once in a while.

**YOU'RE OVER THE HILL WHEN...**

You have a very special comfortable chair from which it is very difficult to remove you.

# YOU'RE OVER THE HILL WHEN...

You look at the menu before looking at the waitress or waiter.

**YOU'RE OVER THE HILL WHEN...**

You start arranging your hair rather than just combing it. Your bathroom is filled with exotic shaped bottles promising all sorts of miracles with your hair. None of them work.

# YOU'RE OVER THE HILL WHEN...

It takes you days to find suits that show enough skin while covering all the bad parts. You've reached a level of maturity that allows you to ignore short-lived fashion fads.

# YOU'RE OVER THE HILL WHEN...

You feel most comfortable straddling two lanes.

# YOU'RE OVER THE HILL WHEN...

You've tried every diet and exercise gadget that comes along and still you gain weight. You eat much less than ever before in your life but it doesn't help.

# YOU'RE
# OVER
# THE
# HILL
### WHEN...

You actually read most of the magazines you have subscriptions to.

# YOU'RE OVER THE HILL WHEN...

Photographs lie to you. Photos and videos show a totally different person than the one you look at in the mirror each morning. The photos show wrinkles and bald spots, sags and age that an honest mirror never turns up.

**YOU'RE OVER THE HILL WHEN...**

No one cares anymore about what you did in high school.

# YOU'RE OVER THE HILL WHEN...

You no longer apologize for your gay or weird friends.

## YOU'RE OVER THE HILL WHEN...

You're an animal until you've had your morning coffee. A morning without coffee is worse than constipation. You're not sure you are a member of the human race until you've had a big cupful.

# YOU'RE OVER THE HILL WHEN...

You are resigned to the fact that certain foods just aren't compatible with your gastrointestinal system.

# YOU'RE OVER THE HILL WHEN...

The stress of having dinner with little kids is only a nostalgic memory.
Grandchildren, of course, are fine for a day or two.

# YOU'RE OVER THE HILL WHEN...

You find yourself squinting during candlelight dinners.

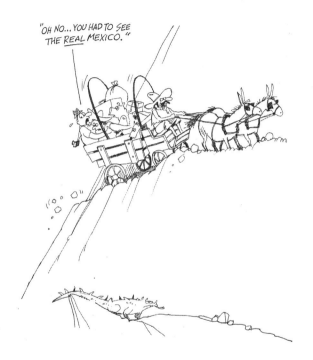

# YOU'RE OVER THE HILL WHEN...

You prefer vacations that involve hot showers and flush toilets. You also prefer places that don't require inoculations for weird diseases.

# YOU'RE OVER THE HILL WHEN...

Your family and friends have finally identified you as the mystery farter.

**YOU'RE OVER THE HILL WHEN...**

You feel like the morning after and you can swear
you haven't been anywhere.

# YOU'RE OVER THE HILL WHEN...

You always look forward to changing into something loose and soft. You no longer discard out-of-style clothes because you know they usually come back. You remember that your father always wore a hat.

**YOU'RE OVER THE HILL WHEN...**

You're smart enough to hire a kid to mow the lawn and shovel the snow.

# YOU'RE OVER THE HILL WHEN...

Just when you were starting to learn the names of all those funny African countries, Eastern Europe and the Soviet Union split apart into even more unpronounceable little places. You have no intention of learning them until they settle down.

# YOU'RE OVER THE HILL WHEN...

Partying involves baked brie and white wine a lot more than waking up with your head in the toilet.

# YOU'RE OVER THE HILL WHEN...

You can't fool your stomach with a pastrami sandwich or cream pie just before bedtime.

**YOU'RE OVER THE HILL WHEN...**

You no longer throw out your too wide or too narrow neckties, knowing they will eventually come back into style.

# YOU'RE OVER THE HILL WHEN...

Having sex is more like Thanksgiving than the Fourth of July.

# YOU'RE OVER THE HILL WHEN...

You have the maturity to realize that any really good presents are going to have to be bought by yourself.

# YOU'RE OVER THE HILL WHEN...

You start reading the ads for hemorrhoids, constipation and hair loss remedies. Worse, you start buying the stuff.

## YOU'RE OVER THE HILL WHEN...

You finally learn to use your bifocals, though going down steps or reading small print up high is still pretty dicey. Usually you can see fine, provided the light is good, but you no longer laugh at the idea of large print books.

# YOU'RE OVER THE HILL WHEN...

You have trouble finding your kind of music on the radio.

**YOU'RE OVER THE HILL WHEN...**

You act your age... most of the time.

# YOU'RE OVER THE HILL WHEN...

You don't take any crap from sales clerks. You can calmly handle most of life's emergencies. Surly waiters, phone solicitors, and incompetent sales help are a piece of cake for you.

**YOU'RE OVER THE HILL WHEN...**

Pretty much everything you own is paid for. You can finally afford lots of things that you no longer want.

# YOU'RE OVER THE HILL WHEN...

You don't go to nude beaches.

# YOU'RE OVER THE HILL WHEN...

You no longer bounce checks.

# YOU'RE OVER THE HILL WHEN...

You are more and more willing to experiment with unusual foods. Pizza and hamburger have given way to yogurt and tofu (did you know that tofu means "whale snot" in Japanese?). You carry antacid pills everywhere you go.

# YOU'RE OVER THE HILL WHEN...

You still pursue members of the opposite sex but you can't quite remember why.

# YOU'RE OVER THE HILL WHEN...

You leave programming the VCR to people under 25. You wonder if you can stall becoming computer literate until retirement. If you memorize a few key computer buzz words, would it fool the "kids" at work?

**YOU'RE OVER THE HILL WHEN...**

You meet old friends and you tell each other "You haven't changed a bit."

# YOU'RE OVER THE HILL WHEN...

You see your old cereal bowl in an antique shop.

**YOU'RE OVER THE HILL WHEN...**

You know where all your warranties are. Unfortunately, you probably can't find your glasses so you can read them.

# YOU'RE OVER THE HILL WHEN...

You never run out of toilet paper.

# YOU'RE OVER THE HILL WHEN...

You absolutely love X-rated movies. You probably have started experimenting with a few sex aids.

# YOU'RE OVER THE HILL WHEN...

There are no longer cartoons and report cards on your refrigerator door.

**YOU'RE OVER THE HILL WHEN...**

You've resigned yourself to never owning that big waterfront lot or a helicopter or achieving some great artistic or scientific accomplishment. And you don't mind much because you're pretty satisfied just as you are.

# YOU'RE OVER THE HILL WHEN...

Everybody has already heard all your jokes.

**YOU'RE OVER THE HILL WHEN...**

You plan ahead to be able to read menus in candlelit restaurants. You learn to avoid places with menus printed in small red type on a maroon background.

# YOU'RE OVER THE HILL WHEN...

You remember to stop the newspapers before going on vacation.

**YOU'RE OVER THE HILL WHEN...**

Not only do you have trouble going upstairs, but when you get there, you may have forgotten what you went upstairs for.

# YOU'RE OVER THE HILL WHEN...

You don't care nearly as much about what people think of your dress or behavior. You've pretty much adopted a style you like and people can go to hell if they don't like it.

**YOU'RE OVER THE HILL WHEN...**

You recognize that middle-age spread only serves to bring people closer together.

# YOU'RE OVER THE HILL WHEN...

Your biological urges may be slowing a bit but you're just as interested in looking as ever. If you're a man, you don't wake up "aroused" everyday.

**YOU'RE OVER THE HILL WHEN...**

You're smart enough not to take out all the garbage in one trip.

# YOU'RE OVER THE HILL WHEN...

You no longer brag about how many parking tickets you have.

**YOU'RE OVER THE HILL WHEN...**

You no longer can sleep until noon.
Probably you can't sleep much past dawn.

# YOU'RE OVER THE HILL WHEN...

You can't remember when prunes, bran and figs weren't a regular part of your diet.

You become an expert on the weather. You watch the weather channel and carefully plan your attire for the expected conditions. You advise all your distant friends and relatives exactly what the weather is in <u>their</u> city.

# YOU'RE OVER THE HILL WHEN...

You have achieved the ability, through long years of practice, to totally and at any time tune out your marriage partner.

# YOU'RE OVER THE HILL WHEN...

You keep forgetting. No matter how many calendars and appointment books you have, you still forget. You write notes on slips of paper and then forget where you put the slips.

# YOU'RE OVER THE HILL WHEN...

Sometimes you stop to think and forget to start again.

# YOU'RE OVER THE HILL WHEN...

You can't remember when things like bran and fiber weren't a regular part of your diet. Your personal plumbing needs more and more stimulation from various heavily advertised regulating remedies.

# YOU'RE
# OVER
# THE
# HILL
## WHEN...

All the prescriptions you never threw out overwhelm your
medicine cabinet.

# YOU'RE OVER THE HILL WHEN...

Reunions with friends or old neighbors are really emotionally poignant occasions. You're pretty sure some of the reminiscences are actually better than the originals. You even start to enjoy family get-togethers.

# YOU'RE OVER THE HILL WHEN...

Your stomach gets upset if you eat raw cookie dough.

You spend less and less time between visits to a toilet. You stop more often on car trips, and frequently make nighttime pilgrimages.

# YOU'RE
# OVER
# THE
# HILL
## WHEN...

There is no stopping the growth of hair in your ears and nose or on your chest and chin. You finally realize you've stopped growing taller though there is plenty of expansion sideways. There's no growth, however, on your head.

**YOU'RE OVER THE HILL WHEN...**

Your arms are barely long enough to hold your reading material.

# YOU'RE OVER THE HILL WHEN...

You hurt after participating in almost any physical activity. Often you hurt after doing absolutely nothing at all. You're glad to read that taking aspirin also prevents various horrible diseases because you swallow an awful lot of them.

**YOU'RE OVER THE HILL WHEN...**

A hair on your head is worth two in the brush.

# YOU'RE OVER THE HILL WHEN...

Some of the junk you threw out after the last garage sale are now collector's items. You can finally afford all the things you no longer want.

# YOU'RE OVER THE HILL WHEN...

You're resigned to being slightly overweight after trying every diet that has come along in the last 15 years.

# YOU'RE OVER THE HILL WHEN...

Driving on dark rainy nights is something you try to avoid. You notice your kids hesitate before driving with you.

**YOU'RE OVER THE HILL WHEN...**

You sit down to put on your underwear. Other people have brightly colored shorts but yours are all white.

# YOU'RE OVER THE HILL WHEN...

Your bookshelf may be overflowing with "How To" and "Self Help" books, but you have pretty well decided that you like yourself just the way you are.

**YOU'RE OVER THE HILL WHEN...**

You remember to call girls "women" about half of the time.

# YOU'RE OVER THE HILL WHEN...

You've reached some sort of accord with your maker even if it's only to add "God willing" to the end of most of your statements.

# YOU'RE OVER THE HILL WHEN...

You always pay your phone and electric bills before they are due.

# YOU'RE
# OVER
# THE
# HILL
## WHEN...

You've gotten very, very good at your job. You even have started to make some real contributions in your field.

**YOU'RE OVER THE HILL WHEN...**

You tend to repeat yourself. All the stories of your athletic exploits as a youth, army adventures, great romances, insightful predictions, and noble gestures have already bored most acquaintances several times over. Unfortunately you can't quite remember telling these stories to everyone, so you repeat them whenever the opportunity arises.

# YOU'RE OVER THE HILL WHEN...

You take your morning bathroom routine very seriously and do not like to be rushed.

You start looking forward to dull evenings at home.

# YOU'RE OVER THE HILL WHEN...

You never really had the chance to get used to guys with long hair or earrings. Sometimes you have trouble doing your business at times like this.

# YOU'RE OVER THE HILL WHEN...

You worry about the long term effects of the sun on your skin, but still love a tan.

# YOU'RE OVER THE HILL WHEN...

You start dressing for comfort. Your color coordination takes a back seat to expediency.

You don't drive like a tiger anymore. Then again, you also don't get speeding tickets or have your car towed. You find the sight of a policeman rather comforting.

# YOU'RE OVER THE HILL WHEN...

The years skip by at a capricious pace and if the next five years pass as quickly as the last, you'll be too old to drive sometime next week.

You stop looking forward to birthdays. You plot revenge on people who give you gifts like this book.

You may send directly to us for the books below. Postage is $1.50 for the first book and $0.50 for each additional book.

## TRADE PAPERBACK BOOKS $5.95

| | |
|---|---|
| 2400 | Sex On Your Birthday |
| 2402 | Confessions From Bathroom |
| 2403 | Good Bonking Guide |
| 2404 | Sex Slave |
| 2405 | Mid-Life Sex |
| 2406 | World's Sex Records |
| 2407 | 40 Happens |
| 2408 | 30: The Big Three-Oh |
| 2409 | 50 Happens |
| 2411 | Geriatric Sex Guide |
| 2412 | Golf Shots |
| 2415 | Birthdays Happen |
| 2416 | Absolutely Worst Fart |
| 2417 | Women Over 30 Are Better |
| 2418 | 9 Months in Sac |
| 2419 | Cucumbers Are Better |
| 2421 | Honeymoon Guide |
| 2422 | Eat Yourself Healthy |
| 2423 | Sex After 40? |
| 2424 | Sex After 50? |
| 2425 | Women Over 40 Are Better |
| 2426 | Women Over 50 Are Better |
| 2427 | Over The Hill |
| 2428 | Beer Is Better |
| 2429 | Married to a Computer |
| 2430 | Sex After 30? |
| 2431 | Happy B'day Old Fart |
| 2432 | Big Weenies |
| 2433 | Games Play With Pussy |
| 2434 | Sex And Marriage |
| 2435 | Baby's First Year |
| 2436 | How To Love A New Yorker |
| 2437 | The Retirement Book |
| 2438 | Dog Farts |
| 2439 | Handling His Mid-Life Crisis |
| 2440 | How To Love A Texan |
| 2441 | Bedtime Stories...Kitty |
| 2442 | Bedtime Stories...Doggie |
| 2443 | 60 With Sizzle! |
| 2444 | The Wedding Night |
| 2445 | Woman's Birthday Wish |
| 2446 | The PMS Book |
| 2447 | The Pregnant Father |
| 2448 | Games Play In Bed |
| 2449 | The Barf Book |
| 2450 | How To Pick Up Girls |
| 2451 | How To Pick Up Guys |
| 2452 | Driving Amongst Idiots |
| 2453 | Beginner's Sex Manual |
| 2454 | Get Well |
| 2455 | Unspeakably Rotten Cartoons |
| 2456 | For A Million Bucks... |
| 2457 | Hooters |
| 2458 | Adult Connect the Dots |
| 2459 | Once Upon A Mattress |
| 2460 | Golfing Amongst Idiots |
| 2461 | Marry Me, Marry Me |
| 2462 | Smokers Are People, Too |

## FUN BOOKS $3.00

| | |
|---|---|
| 2026 | Games Play In Bed |
| 2034 | You're Over 40 When... |
| 2042 | Cucumbers Are Better |
| 2064 | Wedding Night |
| 2067 | It's Time To Retire When... |
| 2068 | Sex Manual...Over 30 |
| 2102 | You're Over 50 When... |
| 2127 | Your Golf Game |
| 2131 | The Fart Book |
| 2136 | The Shit List |
| 2148 | Dear Teacher |
| 2166 | Survived Catholic School |
| 2177 | You're Over The Hill |
| 2180 | Italian Sex Manual |
| 2181 | Jewish Sex Manual |
| 2192 | You're Over 30 When... |
| 2195 | Beer Is Better |
| 2203 | The Last Fart Book |
| 2205 | Sex After 40? |
| 2210 | Sex After Marriage? |
| 2213 | Women Over 50 Are Better |
| 2217 | Sex After 50? |
| 2224 | Life's A Picnic...Big Weenie |
| 2225 | Women Over 40 Are Better |
| 2226 | C.R.S. |
| 2227 | Happy Birthday/Year Older |
| 2229 | You're A Redneck |
| 2233 | Small Busted Women |
| 2234 | You're Over 60 |
| 2235 | You Know You're Over 70 |
| 2236 | Nose Picker's Guide |
| 2237 | 55 & Picking Up Speed |
| 2240 | Dumb Men Jokes |
| 2241 | Cats Are Better Than Men |
| 2242 | Working Woman's Doodle |
| 2243 | Working Man's Doodle |
| 2244 | Words of Wisdom |
| 2245 | Potty Potpourri |

## HARDCOVER BOOKS $8.95

| | |
|---|---|
| 2350 | Sailing |
| 2351 | Computers |
| 2352 | Cats |
| 2353 | Tennis |
| 2354 | Bowling |
| 2355 | Parenting |
| 2356 | Fitness |
| 2357 | Golf |
| 2358 | Fishing |
| 2359 | Bathrooms |
| 2360 | Biking |
| 2361 | Running |
| 2362 | Skiing |
| 2363 | Doctors |
| 2364 | Lawyers |
| 2365 | Teachers |
| 2366 | Nurses |
| 2367 | Firefighters |
| 2368 | Marines |

**Ivory Tower Publishing Co., Inc.,** 125 Walnut St., P.O. Box 9132, Watertown, MA 02272-9132   Tel: (617) 923-1111